ATTINGHAM PARK

Shropshire

THE NATIONAL TRUST

Acknowledgements

This new guidebook has been written by Belinda Cousens, formerly Assistant Historic Buildings Representative and Property Manager responsible for Attingham Park.

Photographs: Country Life Picture Library p. 5; Courtauld Institute of Art p. 40; © Estate of Walter R. Sickert 2000. All rights reserved, DACS. National Trust Photographic Library/John Hammond p. 14 (bottom right); National Trust pp. 4 (left), 10 (bottom right), 26, 41 (top), 44, 50 (top), 51 (top and bottom), 52 (left), 53; NT/Mark Fiennes pp. 8, 18, 19, 21, 30, 31, 35; NT/Cliff Guttridge pp. 24, 32, 33; National Trust Photographic Library p. 54; NTPL/Matthew Antrobus p. 45 (top); NTPL/Oliver Benn p. 22; NTPL/John Bethell pp. 28, 29 (top and bottom); NTPL/John Hammond pp. 4 (right), 6, 9 (top right), 15, 17 (bottom right), 20, 23 (bottom left), 34, 39, 41 (bottom), 42 (top and bottom), 43, 45 (bottom), 47, 48 (left and right), 49 (top and bottom), 52 (right), 55, back cover; NTPL/Angelo Hornak pp. 13 (bottom right), 14 (top left), 50 (bottom); NTPL/James Mortimer front cover, pp. 1, 3, 7, 9 (bottom left), 11, 12, 13 (top left), 16, 17 (top left), 23 (bottom right), 25, 27; NTPL/Derrick E. Witty pp. 4 (centre), 10 (top left), 46; NTPL/Mike Williams p. 36.

© 2000 The National Trust
Registered charity no. 205846
ISBN 1-84359-067-0
Revised 2003, 2004

Typeset from disc and designed by James Shurmer

Print managed by Centurion Press Ltd (BAS) for the National Trust (Enterprises) Ltd, 36 Queen Anne's Gate, London SW1H 9AS

(*Front cover*) The chimneypiece in the Boudoir

(*Title-page*) The Boudoir ceiling

(*Back cover*) Detail of the mosaic top to the gilt table in the Picture Gallery

(*Opposite*) Detail from the Dining Room ceiling

CONTENTS

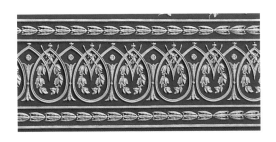

ATTINGHAM PARK

The pleasures and pitfalls of wealth

THE GREAT PORTICO through which you enter Attingham dominates not only this façade, but also the view of the house from across the park. Such was the intention of the man for whom it was built in 1782–5 – NOEL HILL, 1st LORD BERWICK. Though he acquired his title only in 1784, for services rendered to the government of William Pitt, he came from a well-established Shropshire family. Indeed, in building on this scale one of his aims was to outshine his cousins in the senior branch of the Hill family at Hawkstone, north of Shrewsbury.

The house may look big, but it was once even bigger. For Lord Berwick decided not to demolish the existing house, Tern Hall, but to wrap round it another, more fashionable building, which he christened Attingham Park. His architect, George Steuart, a former assistant and rival of Robert Adam, came up with a symmetrical plan with matching suites of rooms of increasing intimacy on either side of the Entrance Hall – for Lord Berwick to the left, and for his wife, Anne, to the right. The servants' quarters in the basement below were segregated by sex in the same way. Tern Hall was demolished about 1856, leaving an open courtyard in the centre of the house.

The 1st Lord Berwick died young in 1789, and it was his eldest son who completed and furnished this vast new mansion. It was a task for which the 2nd LORD BERWICK was ideally suited. Indeed, his chief pleasure in life lay in buying and commissioning works of art, both at home and abroad, which he displayed in his new Picture Gallery at Attingham. But the family motto proved all too apt: 'Wealth is a blessing to those who use it wisely, but a curse to those who don't.' For the result of his extravagance was bankruptcy and led to the sale of almost the entire contents of Attingham in 1827. The house was leased to his brother, William, who became the 3rd LORD BERWICK shortly afterwards. He had been a diplomat in Italy for some 25 years and brought to Attingham the collections of Italian furniture, paintings and diplomatic silver which so enrich the interiors today.

The 3rd Lord Berwick died a bachelor, and the estate passed to the third brother, Richard, who was rector on the estate. By this time, the family could scarcely afford to live in this great house, which as a result was left empty for periods during the latter half of the 19th century. However, the marriage of the 8th LORD BERWICK in 1919 to TERESA HULTON, brought together two people who shared an enthusiasm for the fine and decorative arts, and together they set about the task of renewing and enhancing the interiors. It was their shared concern for the future of Attingham and its collections that led to their decision to give the property to the National Trust, which came about following the death of Lord Berwick in 1947.

(Opposite) Teresa Hulton on the portico steps in 1920, the year after her marriage to the 8th Lord Berwick. The Berwicks revived the house after a period of decline and ensured its preservation

(Far left) Noel, 1st Lord Berwick built the house

(Left, centre) Thomas, 2nd Lord Berwick created the Picture Gallery

(Left) William, 3rd Lord Berwick introduced Old Master paintings and French Neo-classical furniture

TOUR OF THE HOUSE

THE ENTRANCE HALL

Visitors arriving in muddy outdoor clothes would have sat waiting on the robust hall-chairs. The stone floor was designed to withstand hunting boots and constant comings and goings. The decoration contains a symbolic welcome: Mercury, God of Travellers, appears in the right-hand niche.

Behind the vast portico of Steuart's splendid new building, the Entrance Hall may seem something of an anti-climax. In fact, his original scheme of 1785 was both more spacious and amply lit. Opposite the entrance door was an open screen of columns, giving an impressive view to the top-lit central staircase beyond. This was altered 20 years later, when John Nash inserted his great Picture Gallery for the 2nd Lord Berwick, taking the place of three staircases.

The green scagliola (imitation marble) columns and pilasters are original to Steuart's scheme, but the marbled paintwork is part of the later Regency decoration. In 1827 the floor with its massive slabs of Grinshill stone was covered by an oil cloth in a 'stone and slate colour octagon panelled roset pattern', which survived until about 1900. A replica floor cloth was created and installed in 2000

The white marble fireplace is inlaid with scagliola decoration. A second fireplace, which originally stood opposite, was replaced by the staircase to the basement in 1805.

PICTURES

The four grisaille (monochrome) overdoors are by Robert Fagan, an Irish artist-dealer-diplomat who acted on behalf of many English travellers to Rome and Naples. These and another set in the Outer Library must have been specially commissioned by the 2nd Lord Berwick when in Naples in 1793.

The Entrance Hall as originally designed by Steuart, with an open screen of columns and a central staircase

The Entrance Hall. The figure in the niche to the left of the fireplace, painted to resemble sculpture, is Mercury, God of Travellers

IN NICHES OPPOSITE ENTRANCE:

The two figures, also in grisaille, are part of the Regency decorative scheme. They represent Minerva, Goddess of Wisdom, and Mercury, the God of Travellers, both frequently found in decorative schemes for entrance halls.

SCULPTURE

Bust of William Pitt the Younger. He was Prime Minister between 1783 and 1806, and the Berwicks owed their title to him. This bust by Nollekens was taken from Pitt's death-mask in 1806.

FURNITURE

Set of eight hall-chairs in mahogany with the crest of the Hills of Hawkstone in painted roundels. They are of a pattern designed *c.*1790 by Gillows of Lancaster.

Victorian octagonal letter-box in mahogany with acorn finial.

The Drawing Room is the first of the principal rooms on the 'female' side of the house

THE DRAWING ROOM

'In the ravishingly beautiful yet slightly distressed apartment Lord and Lady Berwick were sitting bolt upright talking to each other.... Lady Berwick rose from a stiff settee in a rather stately manner.'

James Lees-Milne, 1936

This is the first of the rooms along the feminine wing of Steuart's symmetrical plan, which was influenced by the French fashion for male and female suites of rooms. It was probably still unfinished when the 1st Lord Berwick died in 1789; the ceiling roundels are empty even now, and the installation of the fireplace was completed only in 1799.

In 1799 the 2nd Lord Berwick, whose portrait hangs over the fireplace, began the task of both completing and updating the furnishing of the new house. Inspired by the French fashion being set by the Prince of Wales at Carlton House, he had the gilt fillets added to the walls, and much of his furniture was in rosewood or gilt. With crimson silk curtains, crimson carpet and red walls, the room would have looked startlingly different.

The present scheme is owed largely to two generations: the 3rd Lord Berwick, who took over the house after the 1827 bankruptcy sale; and the 8th Lord and Lady Berwick, who restored it in the 1920s. The blue walls and lighter colours of the ceiling were probably introduced with the Italian furniture by the 3rd Lord Berwick.

The white marble fireplace, by John Deval the Younger, was ordered in 1785. The central relief shows *Beauty governed by Reason and rewarded by Merit*, from an engraving after Angelica Kauffman of 1783.

CHANDELIER

The ormolu (gilt bronze)-framed glass chandelier with two tiers of nine lights is of a Regency design. The chandelier listed here in the 1827 sale catalogue had a remarkable 36 lights.

TEXTILES

The upholstery of the Italian furniture is due to the last Lady Berwick, who reused old silks found in store, including the unusual painted silk, which was originally made up in fringed panels as wall-hangings.

The blue silk curtains were commissioned by the 8th Lord Berwick, who ordered the silk from Lyons in 1911, when still a bachelor. The silk was copied from the hangings of a French Empire bed Lord Berwick bought in Paris.

The fitted Wilton carpet with matching hearth-rug was probably laid by the 3rd Lord Berwick in the 1830s.

Caroline Murat, for whom some of the Drawing Room furniture may have been made; painted by Louis Ducis

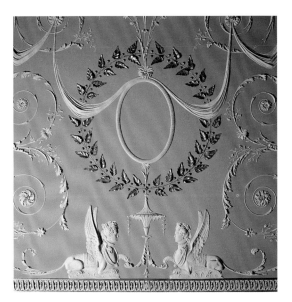

Steuart planned to fill the oval medallions with decoration, but his Adam-style ceiling was never finished

PICTURES

The pictures were mostly bought by the 2nd and 3rd Lords Berwick in Italy. When in Rome in 1792, the 2nd Lord Berwick sat to the Neo-classical painter Angelica Kauffman for his portrait, which hangs over the fireplace. At the same time he commissioned from her the two flanking classical subjects on the theme of love lost (on the right) and found (left), which retain their original Maratta frames and have always hung in this position.

BESIDE ENTRANCE:

Portrait of 4th Lord Berwick in chalk, 1847, by John Hayter. He was vicar of Berrington for many years, despite his stutter and fondness for drink.

The four overdoors are by Philipp Hackert, a German painter working in Naples, who was patronised by both the 2nd and 3rd Lords Berwick.

On the end wall is a portrait of Caroline Murat, the sister of Napoleon and briefly Queen of Naples.

Love lost and found: Angelica Kauffman's Bacchus and Ariadne *depicts the god of wine (with his vine-wreathed staff) coming upon the distraught Ariadne, who had been abandoned by Theseus on the island of Naxos*

SCULPTURE

The full-length figure of *Venus Itálica,* after the great Neo-classical sculptor Antonio Canova, was bought in 1926. It was commissioned in 1816 by Colonel Norcliffe, the original version having been completed in 1811. Canova's workshop was in Asolo, where the last Lady Berwick was born.

The Head of a Dancer, again after Canova, was also bought by the 8th Lord and Lady Berwick and at that time was thought to have been a portrait of Pauline Borghese, Caroline Murat's sister. The original version of this head was presented by Canova to the Duke of Wellington in 1816 in recognition of the Duke's role in returning works of art taken from Rome by Napoleon.

FURNITURE

The white and gold Italian furniture is made up of several part-sets, including armchairs and stools re-upholstered by Lady Berwick. Outstanding are:

The gilt day-bed, reupholstered in pale eau-de-Nil damask, bears the initials CM on a panel over the arm and is linked to Caroline Murat, from whose palace in Naples it may have been acquired by the 3rd Lord Berwick.

A gilt armchair on supports of linked satyrs' legs is in the style of Giocondo Albertolli, a Milanese furniture maker who published his designs in 1796.

A tall-backed gilt armchair with shield-shaped back is particularly striking and may have been the 3rd Lord Berwick's ambassadorial throne.

A pair of Louis XV encoigneurs (corner cupboards), bearing the stamp of M. CRIAERD, a maker known for his flamboyant marquetry.

Caroline Murat in the Palazzo Belvedere in Naples with some of the Neo-classical furniture now at Attingham; watercolour by F. Macdonald

Antonio Canova's Venus Italica *in the Drawing Room*

Small occasional table in cherrywood, French, *c.*1810, the tripod base with curved legs surmounted by sphinx busts.

The brass inlaid rosewood side-tables at both ends of the room, with their accompanying mirrors and those on the window wall, are part of the original Regency furnishings and were made by Thomas Donaldson of Shrewsbury.

MUSICAL INSTRUMENT

A pianoforte in satinwood case by Collard & Collard, 1836.

The green lacquered music stand and stool with painted Neo-classical decoration may have been supplied by Erard, *c.*1812.

CLOCK

Two-day French ormolu and marble case mantel clock by Pierre Gregson, an Englishman working in Paris in the 1780s. Its five concentric hands indicate the second, minute, hour, day of the week and month.

THE SULTANA ROOM

This room, with its view across the river to the deer-park, was most often used by the family in the early 20th century, and many visitors were entertained to tea here by the last Lady Berwick. The silver tea service was presented to her and Lord Berwick by the estate tenants in 1919 in celebration of their marriage.

The room takes its name from the alcove with its Ottoman settee, or 'Sultane', illustrating the Regency period's free adoption of exotic influences. A design in a Gillows notebook dated 1813 shows that the alcove was then framed with richly tasselled drapery in the style of the window curtains opposite. This is one of the few rooms where the Regency silk survives, and the curtains and upholstery were extensively patched or over-stitched by the last Lady Berwick and her helpers. She

continued the 18th-century practice of covering the silk upholstery with cotton covers for everyday use, thus prolonging the life of the silk.

This room and the Boudoir beyond were probably completed before the 1st Lord Berwick died in 1789. Steuart's ceiling design, in the style of his former employer, Robert Adam, uses the symbols of Cupid – the arrow and torches – to convey the theme of love. The painted roundels, from designs of the 1770s by Angelica Kauffman, also illustrate scenes from the life of Cupid. The room was originally hung with green silk.

PICTURES

The group of portraits on the wall opposite the fireplace includes the first Lady Berwick holding her baby son, Thomas, who was born here in 1770, and a pastel portrait of one of her sisters, Miss Vernon, both attributed to William Hoare of Bath.

The Sultana Room takes its name from the sofa or 'sultane' in the alcove

A gilt musical box decorated with a monkey conducting a harp

SCULPTURE

The painted plaster bust of 'Flora' is by the French sculptor J.-B. Carpeaux and derives from the relief he sculpted for a pediment on the Louvre in Paris in 1874; purchased by the 8th Lord Berwick.

MUSICAL INSTRUMENT

A double-action 'Grecian' harp by Erard, in gilded gesso and black lacquer.

FURNITURE

Two massive gilt-framed mirrors over the fireplace and on the window wall are replacements of *c.*1830 for those sold in 1827.

*The French marble-topped mahogany commode, c.*1780, may be the one purchased by the 8th Lord Berwick in Paris before the First World War, when much of the French furniture was acquired.

Gilt tripod torchère (candlestand), *c.*1800, with amboyna wood top and base.

Lady's work-table in mahogany and coromandel (Chinese lacquer) veneer, from a design by Sheraton published in his *Cabinet-Maker, Upholsterer and General Artist's Encyclopaedia* (1805).

The lady's painted cabinet on stand illustrates the type of decorated piece that might have furnished this room in the 1780s; possibly painted by George Brookshaw.

French marquetry chest-of-drawers (semainier) with seven drawers and an additional one in the frieze, *c.*1830.

CLOCKS

Eight-day French mantel clock, ormolu case with two putti blowing bubbles, *c.*1830.

Eight-day French mantel clock in ormolu and green marble case by Lesage of Paris, *c.*1830.

CERAMICS

A pair of baluster vases in the style of Chinese export ware, possibly by Emile Samson, *c.*1880. The coat of arms belongs to the Howard family.

William Hoare of Bath's pastel probably portrays one of the 1st Lord Berwick's sisters-in-law

A pastel by Lady Berwick's father, William Hulton, of their home in Venice

THE EAST ANTE-ROOM

After the last war, this became the Berwicks' dining-room, and much of the furniture and picture collection here was acquired by them.

PICTURES

To the left of the fireplace is a portrait of the last Lady Berwick painted at Attingham by Sir Gerald Kelly in 1923. On the wall opposite is another three-quarter length portrait of her painted in 1933 by Walter Sickert, a friend of the family who used to paint with her father in Venice.

Alongside this portrait hang four small paintings by Lady Berwick's father, William Hulton, including a *View of Asolo* where Lady Berwick was born, and an interior view of their Venetian home in the Palazzo Dona with her sister Gioconda seated. Here

(Right) Teresa, Lady Berwick by Sickert in 1933 as Lady in Blue. *'No one could call it a portrait,' she said, 'it is a fantasia in a characteristic subdued colour scheme.' But in fact it does catch her likeness*

Mount Vesuvius by Moonlight: The Eruption of
1787; by Giovanni Battista Lusieri

the Hultons entertained Henry James and Robert
Browning, among others.

On the window wall are two watercolours purchased by the 2nd Lord Berwick in Italy, including
Mount Vesuvius by Moonlight by G. B. Lusieri, showing the eruption of 1787.

FURNITURE

French gilt overmantel mirror in Louis XV style, *c.*1830,
bought by the 8th Lord Berwick.

*Marble-topped mahogany chest-of-drawers, c.*1810, bearing the stamp of the Parisian maker F. H. G. Jacob-
Desmalter, son of the more famous Georges Jacob.

*Mahogany fall-front bureau, c.*1810, also French and
possibly introduced by the 3rd Lord Berwick.

Marble-topped console table in carved oak, French,
*c.*1750, purchased by the 8th Lord Berwick.

MINIATURES

These include the only confirmed portrait of Noel,
1st Lord Berwick, in a scarlet jacket by Jeremiah
Meyer; a group portrait of his three daughters,
Henrietta, Anna and Amelia, by Andrew Plimer;
and the only portrait of Sophia, wife of the 2nd
Lord Berwick, by Richard Cosway.

CLOCK

Eight-day English mantel clock in tortoiseshell and
ormolu case, *c.*1820.

THE BOUDOIR

This is the last and most intimate of the rooms in the female wing of the house. The name comes from the French word *bouder*, 'to sulk'. It must have been designed specifically for Anne Vernon, the 1st Lady Berwick, and may be one of the few rooms to have been completed in the 1780s. Again, the theme of the decoration is Love. The Berwicks seem to have married for love: she was not an heiress, and his family objected to the match.

The painted 'grotesque' decorations are of such extremely fine quality that they have been attributed to Louis-André Delabrière, who worked for the Prince of Wales at Carlton House in 1787 and later at Southill in Bedfordshire. In both cases the architect Henry Holland was overseeing the project, and it has been suggested that Steuart may have trained with Holland, although there is no proof of this. The fashion for this style of decoration had been given fresh impetus by Robert Adam, but derives from Raphael's decorations in the Vatican, as well as from classical models.

The decorative scheme is based on designs of 1775 by Angelica Kauffman, with Cupids in the roundels of the domed ceiling; *Venus guarding the Sleeping Cupid* in the marble roundel surmounting the mantelpiece; and six further scenes in the wall panels. The symmetry of the decorative scheme was

The Boudoir – the climax of the suite of rooms on the 'female' side of the house

Detail of the Boudoir overmantel

enhanced by the textiles, which in 1827 included blue and white damask festooned drapery framing the mirror as well as the window opposite.

Of the five doors, only the two diagonally opposite each other afford access; one is a false door, the other pair encloses cupboards, one of which was fitted out with Gothic alcoves and drawers to accommodate a shell collection, probably that formed by the 1st Lord Berwick's mother. The oak parquet floor was installed in 1952 after an outbreak of dry-rot.

FURNITURE

A surprising quantity of furniture filled this room in 1827: a couch and six matching chairs upholstered in straw-coloured silk with blue cord bindings and a further eight chairs upholstered *en suite* with the curtains. Much of the present furniture was purchased by the 8th Lord Berwick while working in Paris, including the small Aubusson rug.

Set of six painted chairs, Italian in the style of 1810, possibly introduced by the last Lady Berwick.

Pair of French mahogany armchairs in the style of Georges Jacob, purchased by the 8th Lord Berwick.

Lady's writing desk of c.1820, bearing the stamp of the French maker Becker.

Mahogany chair made in High Wycombe for the coronation of Edward VII in 1902. It was customary for guests to have the opportunity to buy their chairs.

CLOCK

Eight-day French mantel clock in ormolu elephant case by Lesage of Paris, c.1850.

THE EAST PASSAGE

This passage runs around the core of the house and enabled servants to reach the private rooms without passing through the state rooms.

WALLPAPER

The two panels of French wallpaper show views of India. They were bought by the 8th Lord Berwick and originally installed in his bathroom on the first floor. The hand-blocked paper was made c.1815 by the Parisian firm Dufour, which specialised in such scenic papers.

PICTURES

Also deriving from Lord Berwick's stay in Paris is the set of lithographs by the Australian artist Charles Conder.

A tiger hunt, from the early 19th-century French scenic wallpaper in the East Passage

THE PICTURE GALLERY

This magnificent room represents one generation's passion for art and music. The 2nd Lord Berwick built it; his brother, the 3rd Lord Berwick, bought most of the pictures now hanging here; and their sister, Henrietta, who was a talented musician, played the organ.

The Picture Gallery was designed in 1805 by John Nash, the architect of the Brighton Pavilion. It was an extraordinarily bold scheme, which illustrates not only the scale of the 2nd Lord Berwick's purchases, both in Italy and in London, but also the inventiveness of his architect. Here Nash makes novel use of cast iron in the curved beams, made at Coalbrookdale, to form the glazed roof. However, the design with its continuous cove gave problems with leaks, and a secondary glazed aluminium-framed roof had to be installed in the 1960s.

The decoration of the room reveals Nash at his most showy, with the porphyry-coloured scagliola

The 1st Lord Berwick's three musical daughters would all have played this organ, which was made in 1788

columns and glossy Chinese vermilion walls set off by gilt capitals and mouldings to the walls and ceiling, the brilliant white marble fireplaces and a rich inlaid floor. Analysis of the paintwork has revealed that the room has always been painted this deep red, given additional depth by a glaze. During the 18th century, red in a variety of shades had become the favoured colour on which to display Old Masters, a taste which was reinforced at the end of the century by the archaeological discoveries at Herculaneum and Pompeii. Beneath the cornice a gilt fringe disguises the line of the picture rail.

CARPET

In 1827, the carpet was a crimson red, but the 3rd Lord Berwick subsequently chose an indigo blue. When the Trust had to renew the carpet recently, the decision was made to opt for a blue carpet again, because the pictures and furniture now in the room largely represent the 3rd Lord Berwick's collection. By a stroke of luck some pieces of the old blue carpet were found inside the organ, which was being restored at the time.

PICTURES

The few paintings from the 2nd Lord Berwick's collection which remain at Attingham were bought in at the 1827 sale by the 3rd Lord Berwick. Only a little of the latter's own collection has escaped similar sales in his lifetime. There were further sales in the 20th century, so the present hang cannot represent a historical arrangement. However, the pictures are hung in the traditional manner, in symmetrical groups and in up to four tiers. The north-facing wall comprises mainly the work of northern artists, including, most notably, the two large views of Pompeii and Lake Avernus by Philipp Hackert. This pair was commissioned by the 2nd Lord Berwick, but his brother also collected works by Hackert, so that there are nine by him at Attingham today.

In spite of the losses, the collection still illustrates the eclectic taste of early 19th-century collectors, with paintings by 16th- and 17th-century artists alongside contemporary works, portraits and landscapes beside historical paintings, and copies jostling with originals.

MUSICAL INSTRUMENTS

The chamber organ by Samuel Green is dated 1788 and must have been installed initially in another room, probably the Drawing Room. The Sheraton-style case, veneered in mahogany and satinwood and with false gilt pipes, is independent of the organ itself. By this date, private concerts were fashionable and several of Green's organs were supplied for country houses as their light tone makes them especially suited to domestic settings. The three daughters of the 1st Lord Berwick were particularly musical. The eldest, Henrietta, was taught by the pioneer historian of music, Dr Charles Burney, and played the harpsichord, piano and guitar.

FURNITURE

A pair of gilt console tables with Sicilian Jasper tops supported by chimaeras (mythical beasts, part-lion, part-serpent) with coromandel veneer to the frieze and drawers. These were supplied in 1811 by Thomas Donaldson of Shrewsbury, who also provided the gilt enrichments for the Picture Gallery.

A pair of Italian gilt tables, *c.*1800, with mosaic tops and papier-mâché vases for pot-pourri on the stretchers, in the style of Giuseppe Mario Bonzanigo, who worked for the Court at Turin.

Marble-topped table on a white-painted base with gilt decoration. The base was probably made *c.*1830 in England to match the Italian furniture in the house. The early 17th-century Florentine inlaid marble top, was probably brought back from Italy by the 3rd Lord Berwick in the 1830s.

CHANDELIER

A cut-glass chandelier with twelve lights and five tiers of glass drops. It corresponds in some respects with that in the 1827 sale catalogue, and may have been altered when converted to electricity.

THE STAIRCASE

This handsome staircase was meant for show as much as for use. It does not in fact reach the first floor; from the second landing, two jib doors open into tunnel-like flights of steps to complete the distance.

Nash designed it to replace Steuart's central top-lit staircase, which, with two flanking service stairs, occupied the position of the Picture Gallery. The drum-like space is treated with considerable panache, with ribbed plasterwork, which was then a fashionable treatment for rooms of this shape. The fish-scale decoration to the cove of the dome is worthy of the Brighton Pavilion. The quality of the woodwork is superb. The mahogany handrail is inlaid with satinwood and ebony stringing, while the risers to the steps are inlaid with a diaper pattern in satinwood relating to the inlaid border of the Picture Gallery floor.

THE WEST PASSAGE

This passage originally linked to the main rooms of Tern Hall, therefore must have been used regularly by the family. Nevertheless, the decoration is of lower quality, with the doors on the east side painted to resemble mahogany.

ARCHITECTURAL DRAWINGS

The collection of architectural drawings here illustrates the development of Attingham during the 1780s as well as some of Steuart's unexecuted proposals and a view of Tern Hall in 1775. The floor plans show how Steuart proposed to integrate Tern Hall into his new building. Four views of the Entrance Hall serve as a reminder of the greater impact of the original scheme. Also notable of the interior views is that of the Outer Library (*at the far end of the passage*) with the scheme for reefed drapery over the bookcases to protect the books from both dust and sunlight (illustrated on p. 34).

One of George Steuart's designs for the Entrance Hall

The Staircase

THE OCTAGON ROOM

This represents the end of the masculine suite of rooms, balancing the Boudoir on the east side. In the post-war years, it has served as an office.

These rooms were probably not finished at the 1st Lord Berwick's death, which may explain why the second fireplace from the Entrance Hall was moved here about 1807. Nevertheless, the plasterwork of the ceiling certainly belongs to the original scheme, a slightly old-fashioned design but of extraordinarily delicate workmanship. In the Regency scheme, the three rooms on this side were decorated *en suite*, the windows hung with lavish drapery of pink silk with black stamped velvet borders. The silk survives, somewhat darkened, in the lining of some of the bookcases, which were installed in 1813 at the same time as the brass lattice doors.

In the 1890s the Octagon Room was being used as an everyday dining-room, as it was closer to the Kitchen than the Dining Room. It was one of the rooms leased to the various wartime tenants and used as offices, when the modern carpets were installed. In 1947 it became the office of George Trevelyan, warden of the Shropshire Adult College, who equipped it with striking furniture designed and made by himself. (He had been trained in the Gimson school in the Cotswolds.) After the College closed in 1975, this room was redecorated by the leading interior decorator John Fowler.

The Octagon

PICTURES

The portrait over the fireplace is of Richard Cosway, a self-portrait, *c.*1770, believed to be from the 3rd Lord Berwick collection.

FURNITURE

A writing-table in mahogany, *c.*1810, in the style of Antoine-Nicolas Lesage, both a manufacturer and purveyor of furniture in Paris.

Boulle inkstand, signed by Louis Le Gaigneur. The distinctive mastiff, which operates the lock system, suggests that this is the inkstand supplied in 1816 for the Prince of Wales; it may have been given to Lady Broughton, whose collection passed to the 3rd Lord Berwick.

CERAMICS

ON MANTELPIECE:

The group of Wedgwood basaltware, all Neo-classical designs of *c.*1780, was bequeathed to the National Trust by Miss Adam-Smith from the Bessemer Wright Collection.

CLOCKS AND METALWORK

Eight-day English mantel clock in French bronze and ormolu case, *c.*1820. The figures represent Study and Philosophy, designed in 1780 for the Sèvres factory by Louis Simon Boizot, and thereafter much imitated.

Chandelier with an alabaster bowl and six bronze branches, purchased by the 8th Lord Berwick in 1927.

THE WEST ANTE-ROOM

Duelling pistols and fishing rods were kept here in the late 19th century. The room's masculine character is maintained by the display of commemorative jugs celebrating the electoral successes of the family from 1774 to 1907.

CERAMICS

Election jugs: the earliest (bottom left) is a Caughley jug commemorating Noel Hill's election as MP for Shropshire in 1774. The large, damaged, earthenware jug (in centre) records the victory in 1796 of William Hill over his relative Sir John Hill by a majority of 469. This result was achieved only by the mayor subsequently discounting a number of votes in favour of Sir John. The campaign was said to have cost the two families over £100,000 in ale for prospective voters.

A jug celebrating Noel Hill's election victory in 1774

Paris porcelain dessert service by Dagoty, *c.*1813. These are part of a dessert service of over 100 pieces, probably acquired by the 3rd Lord Berwick from the Palazzo Belvedere, the Murats' palace in Naples which he leased in 1825. The battle scenes illustrate Napoleon's Russian campaign of 1812, in which Marshall Murat served. The topographical scenes include the parks at St Cloud, Ermenonville and Monceaux in France.

PICTURES

OPPOSITE DISPLAY CASE:

The set of landscape views are designs by John Nash and A. C. Pugin of *c.*1798 for a picturesque village proposed at the entrance to the park. The terrace of cottages with a Gothic bay window was probably all that was completed, and is identifiable today.

A view of a cottage in the picturesque village planned by John Nash for the entrance to the park

THE INNER LIBRARY

The 2nd Lord Berwick was such a voracious book-buyer that he had to convert this former breakfast-room into a library about 1810, having already fitted out a new library in Tern Hall.

The local furniture-maker Thomas Donaldson submitted bills for installing doors and lattice work to existing shelving in 1812; the West Ante-Room and Octagon were similarly fitted out the following year. The walls were painted their present colour at the same time. The ceiling was restored in Spring 2002 to reveal a decorative scheme thought to be by Nash in the early 1800s.

BOOKS

All the books now here belonged to the family, but they represent only a small fraction of the collection sold in 1827. The 2nd Lord Berwick began his book-buying in Italy and was interested in early manuscripts as well as important contemporary printing. He employed the local bookbinder Eddowes but also commissioned bindings in London, including some by leading German immigrant binders such as Kalthoeber and Walther. The 3rd Lord Berwick (whose portrait hangs opposite the fireplace) also shared his interest, and his library of some 9,000 volumes was sold in London after his death in 1842. However, most of these came from his Hampshire home, and of the few that he

Lord Berwick's bookplate

brought to Attingham, a small group remains in the freestanding cabinets.

The 8th Lord Berwick was also a keen collector of books, particularly examples of modern fine printing and first editions, including Rupert Brooke and Yeats. At the same time, he was selling items from the historic collection, notably all the early manuscripts. His own collection was later sold.

PICTURES

The portraits depict members of the Hill family and their associates.

OVER FIREPLACE:

109 *The Hon. and Rev. Richard Hill*, c.1690. The chief creator of the Hill family's fortune and status in the county.

OPPOSITE FIREPLACE:

The family group of c.1730 by Charles Phillips represents Thomas Hill (1693–1782) with his first wife, Anne Powys, and their children. He inherited the Attingham estate in 1734.

CENTRE OF WINDOW WALL:

70 *Sir Rowland Hill*, ancestor of the Hill family, who was Lord Mayor of London in 1549.

FURNITURE

A rosewood centre-table with brass inlay; a typical Regency piece of c.1810.

A writing-table in Boulle, c.1830.

Set of four mahogany armchairs, with lions'-head terminals to the curved arms, in the style of George Smith, who published his designs in 1808.

Pair of rosewood book cabinets, c.1830, with striking shell mounts in the style of Edward Holmes Baldock.

Pair of globes on mahogany stands, c.1810, with terrestrial and celestial maps by Dudley Adams; a bequest from the Norris Collection.

Boulle glazed cabinet, probably 'the large Boule Armoire' bought by the 3rd Lord Berwick in 1833 for £70.

The Inner Library

THE DINING ROOM

The 1st Lord Berwick, who commissioned this room, enjoyed his food and drink, and suffered from gout as a result. His wife had a delicate stomach, which she tried to cure by sea-bathing.

The climax to the masculine suite of rooms, the Dining Room has the most inventive of Steuart's ceiling designs. The motifs of vines and wheat are typical themes for a dining-room, with their references to Bacchus, the God of Wine, and Ceres, the Goddess of the Harvest, but here they are used with unusual panache. The quality of the plasterwork suggests the work of Joseph Bromfield, a local plasterer who had worked with Thomas Farnolls Pritchard.

As this room is a considerable distance from the kitchen, the family continued to use the old dining-room in Tern Hall. To improve its convenience, the last Lady Berwick had a lift installed in one of the doorways, but, during the last war, used the East Ante-Room as her dining-room. When Edgbaston Girls School was evacuated here from Birmingham in 1939, this became its assembly room, an arrangement continued by the succeeding college tenants. Only with the departure of Concorde College in 1982 was it possible for the National Trust to re-instate this splendid interior as a Regency dining-room. Much of the original furniture had been sold,

but the striking set of chairs survived, and the room still creates an impression similar to that conveyed by Lady Hester Leeke's watercolour of c.1840.

PICTURES

4 *William Hill, 3rd Lord Berwick*, who was a diplomat in Italy for 25 years and brought to Attingham his collections of Italian furniture, paintings, silver and ceramics.

Henrietta Maria Hill, Marchioness of Ailesbury, a daughter of the 1st Lord Berwick, by Sir Thomas Lawrence, in whose studio it remained until his death in 1830.

OVER FIREPLACE:

William Pitt, a copy of the portrait by John Hoppner, which was also a source for Nollekens's posthumous bust of Pitt in the Entrance Hall.

FURNITURE

A set of 24 mahogany dining-chairs, the backs with inset metal panels of vines, similar to a set designed by William Porden for Eaton Hall in Cheshire c.1807.

Mahogany Regency dining-table, c.1810, on five tripod pedestal supports, in the style of Gillows.

Mahogany sideboard, c.1780. One of the few pieces of furniture contemporary with Steuart's building.

The Dining Room about 1840; watercolour by Lady Hester Leeke

METALWORK

A French ormolu table setting, c.1810, by Pierre-Philippe Thomire. Similar to a set supplied to Pauline Borghese now in the British Embassy in Paris. This set may have belonged to her sister, Caroline Murat, and would have been acquired by the 3rd Lord Berwick in Naples.

CERAMICS

The ceramics on the table are more pieces from the dessert service by Dagoty, c.1810, which, like the ormolu above, may have belonged to Caroline Murat.

TEXTILES

A large hand-knotted Axminster rug, c.1800. Although this carpet is admirably suited to the room in terms of colouring, date and quality, it was only introduced about 1920. The original carpet here was a Turkey rug of similar size, and the surrounding boards were protected by a floor-cloth.

Set of woollen and velvet curtains, in the Regency style, copied from the original set, probably designed and made by Gillows in London in 1812, which survived here until 1920. Remnants were found in the house so that the fabrics could be copied and made up following the design shown in Lady Hester Leeke's watercolour (illustrated on p. 26).

Return to the Entrance Hall and take the staircase down to the Basement.

THE SERVANTS' HALL

'He had the travelling trunks repaired, his master's frockcoat cleaned and his silk stockings washed; he paid the subscription to the *Sporting Calendar*, posted letters and bought stationery; he also bought powder, pomatum, a razor strap, a shaving box with soap and a toothbrush.'

The duties of William Bennett, footman, in May 1770

This handsome stone-vaulted room is one of a pair, the second situated in the opposite corner beneath the Drawing Room. These very architectural interiors are unlike any other by Steuart and are reminiscent of Sir John Soane's work at this time. Although designed as a servants' hall in Steuart's layout, by 1827 this had become a menservants' dormitory, with six assorted beds, some probably discarded from the upper rooms as old-fashioned. The Servants' Hall had been moved to the back of the house – a more logical location, near the service courtyard and out of sight and sound of the principal rooms.

In the 1861 inventory, this was again described as the Servants' Hall, with a 20-foot table and six forms, but following the demolition of Tern Hall, a second servants' hall was created in the basement of the west wing. During this period the house was being used only intermittently by the family, and the numbers of living-in servants listed in censuses vary from three to seventeen.

Edgbaston Girls School used this as its diningroom, which it remained during the college tenancy. The adjoining Butler's Pantry was completely gutted and became the servery. Almost all the basement furnishings of Attingham were sold in 1947. The painted dresser, assorted 19th-century Windsor chairs and a handsome Staffordshire blue-and-white dinner service are all generous gifts to the National Trust, without which these basement rooms could not be adequately shown to visitors. The long elm table has recently been returned to Attingham from Wilderhope Manor.

PICTURES

The equestrian portrait of a man in hunting pink is described as of Noel Hill, 1st Lord Berwick, but his widow claimed only one portrait had been made of him, the miniature by Meyer.

The painting of 'Bishop', by the Cheshire artist Thomas Stringer, depicts one of Noel Hill's racehorses.

CLOCK

Eight-day English longcase clock by Jason Cox, London, *c.*1748, in walnut veneered case.

These early 19th-century silver-gilt labels would have been hung round the necks of decanters filled with the appropriate wine

THE VAULTS

This was formerly a well-stocked wine cellar. In 1808 it contained some 400 bottles of sherry, 300 of port, 140 of Madeira, and lesser quantities of numerous spirits and other wines.

SILVER

The magnificent collection of silver now on show here was mostly acquired by William Hill, 3rd Lord Berwick, in the course of his diplomatic career in Italy. As ambassador, he was entitled to a quantity of plate, supplied by the Government so that he could present an appropriate image abroad on behalf of his country. William Hill received 5,833 ounces of white plate and 1,066 of gilt plate 'to be returned on demand', but which he appears to have retained.

The *elegant silver candlesticks* supported by female caryatids are by Richard Cook, 1804.

In the first showcase there is a number of more domestic items, including a *large set of table candlesticks*, an assortment of *wine and sauce labels* and an unusual *travelling candlestick and inkwell*. In silver-gilt there is a *stirrup-cup in the form of a fox's head* by Thomas Pitts, 1769, and an *egg-boiler with timer* made by John Edwards, 1802.

Displayed in the last case is a fine *helmet-shaped ewer* by David Willaume, 1715, bearing the coat of arms of the Hill family, the only major item to have survived the auction of 1827, which included some 185 lots of silver. This case also contains a number of presentation items, including two *Adamstyle racing trophies* by John Creswell, won in 1778, and two handsome *bowls* presented to the 8th Lord Berwick in 1898 on his coming-of-age by the tenants of the estate and the tradesmen of Shrewsbury.

This silver gilt candelabra was made by Paul Storr in 1809 as part of the 3rd Lord Berwick's ambassadorial dinner service

This may have been part of a bargain to persuade him to leave his post at Naples early in order to make way for Lord Palmerston's nephew.

THREE CASES, OPPOSITE DOOR:

The diplomatic plate was supplied by the firm of Rundell, Bridge & Rundell, which employed many of the most notable silversmiths of the period. *The silver dinner service* here, including 96 plates, was designed by Paul Storr, along with the silver-gilt centrepiece, candlesticks and coasters, all made between 1810 and 1820. Of similar date is a pair of finely engraved *silver-gilt fruit dishes* made by Benjamin and James Smith, who also made the *set of wine labels* and *handsome Neo-classical tea service*.

A spirit lamp, made by John Edwards in 1802

THE BASEMENT LOBBIES

The two lobbies in the central basement passage originally contained the two service stairs which ran up the full height of the house, flanking the main staircase, which only linked the principal rooms to the first floor. Two small replacement stone staircases were built in the corners of the Inner Courtyard, which had been designed by Steuart for water-closets. It seems that the loss of the latter was not fully remedied until 1856, as part of the major repairs and improvements initiated by the 5th Lord Berwick.

The bell system was also installed only after 1861, the bedrooms being previously identified by numbers rather than letters. The servants' bedrooms were at the back of the house, so that with the two upper floors of the main house and additional rooms in Tern Hall, the family could command 26 bedrooms.

The Ordnance Survey maps here used as wall-coverings were installed by the College. *Please do not touch them.*

CERAMICS

The remarkable collection of English blue-and-white china displayed here was given in 1991 by Miss Doreen Hunt of Bourne in Lincolnshire. In 1827 the housekeeper's cupboards contained fourteen different services, for breakfast, dinner, tea and supper.

Turn right.

The Basement Passage

THE STEWARD'S ROOM

The name derived from Steuart's plan, but in fact this handsome room quickly became the steward's room, where the steward managed the finances of the house and estate. It has never contained a lot of furniture and may always have been available for occasional staff and tenants' parties. Certainly, when Lady Berwick recalled her first Christmas at Attingham in 1920, she described the tenants' children having a party here and all receiving a present from the Christmas tree.

The great salmon was caught on the estate by Thomas Allen about 1912 at the confluence of the River Tern and the Severn. He was the great-uncle of one of Attingham's present tenants, Richard Adney, and lived at Waters Upton. The fish apparently weighed more than the official record for a salmon, which is held by Miss Ballantine, who caught a 64 lb specimen on the Tay in 1922.

Off this room lie the Housekeeper's Room and her still-room and kitchen. The basement follows the plan of the principal rooms, with the female department under Lady Berwick's rooms and the butler's domain in the basement of the masculine wing. The Housekeeper's Room now

The Steward's Room

houses the Family Activity room. The other two rooms are used as offices, but the Trust hopes to reopen them.

PICTURES

The three portraits of Hereford cattle are of some of the 5th Lord Berwick's prize herd. The group of sporting paintings in mahogany frames is on loan from Davenport House, near Bridgnorth. They are the work of E. W. Gill of the 1820s.

Make your way back down the passage to the kitchens. The house offices which occupy the basement rooms in the west wing formerly housed the Butler's Pantry and Bedroom, and a Footman's Bedroom.

THE KITCHEN

The kitchen was originally in the basement of Tern Hall. When it was demolished in the 1850s, this new kitchen was built slightly closer to the Steuart Dining Room.

Beyond the Kitchen lay the pastry and meat larders, and the scullery, where vegetables were prepared and the washing-up took place. A still-room/kitchen lay in the east wing in the housekeeper's domain, where jams and preserves would have been made and stored. This represents a somewhat reduced establishment, and indeed, even in 1871, when there were seventeen live-in servants, only four relate to the Kitchen: the cook, kitchen maid, dairy maid and still-room maid. Additional help may have been provided from the estate.

With the changes in the use of the house brought by the 20th century, the Kitchen had to be modernised. The old ranges were bricked up, the stone floor was covered with concrete and modern tiles, and much of the plasterwork was renewed. Most dramatically of all, in the 1950s the College built additional student accommodation on to the back of the house and inserted an additional floor across the Kitchen, which previously was twice its present height. It was the intense heat generated by the open ranges that necessitated the great height of the old kitchen, with a second row of windows for ventilation.

With the departure of the College, it was possible to plan the restoration and opening of the Kitchen to visitors. The considerable cost has been offset by a raffle run by Mrs Gwyneth Kern and a generous donation from Shropshire County Hotels. Preliminary excavations revealed that the stone floors survived beneath the concrete, and the two cast-iron ranges were discovered behind a flat wall. Guided by the catalogue and inventories of 1827, 1861, 1898 and 1913, the Trust will continue to re-equip the Kitchen.

FURNITURE

The great kitchen table may be that described in 1827: 'a capital stout elm-topped table, 16 feet × 4 feet 4.' This was split in two and continued to be used in the Kitchen with the addition of Formica tops. The two halves have now been joined together again, and a new elm top fitted. The rest of the old Kitchen furniture was sold in 1947.

Two dressers were listed in the 1913 inventory, with measurements which made it possible to identify their positions from marks on the stone floor. They have been remade, using the surviving table as a pattern.

EQUIPMENT

The central cast-iron open range of c.1830 is set within a stone arch, on which the date 1861 has been found, and may have been transferred from the old kitchen. It was not only for cooking, but also for heating water in the two large rivetted tanks at the back. The width of the grate could be varied by adjusting the cheeks, to control the amount of water heated and coal used. In front of this open range stood a 'hastener', a mobile tin-lined cupboard which acted both as a shield for the heat and a hot cupboard for heating plates and dishes.

The spit mechanism has had to be reproduced; all that survived were the brackets on the range and the evidence of the hole in the wall above. The spit was originally turned by a fan set within the chimney and driven by the rising smoke and heat; it has now been electrified. A large copper drip pan would have stood underneath.

The Kitchen

The Kitchen

THE NEW SERVANTS' HALL (SHOP)

The *Flavel Kitchener* of *c*.1880 probably replaced another piece of equipment when it was installed. Established in 1833 in Leamington, the firm specialised in kitcheners. This range offers considerable flexibility, with its three ovens and several hot-plates designed to produce the complex French-inspired menus then being served in fashionable society.

Batterie de cuisine; in 1861 the full set of copper amounted to over 100 different items, including 30 assorted stew pans and 28 moulds. None of this collection passed to the National Trust, so the pieces now displayed have been acquired by gift and purchase and will be added to. (*Copies of the Kitchen inventories are displayed here.*)

In 1919, when the last Lady Berwick was moving into Attingham, she reported to her mother that there were to be seven servants - 'not much for this barracks'. A new butler and second housemaid had been appointed, and the odd-job man was just starting. Faced with so much to tackle in refurbishing this great house, she commented: 'I wish I were a practical American'.

This room became a servants' hall only following the alterations commissioned in 1856. At this time the wooden floor and fireplace were installed and the windows raised. Previously, this space had been a brick-vaulted larder. The present colour scheme of *c*.1900 was found under wallpapers that had been put up when the room was subdivided in the 1950s to create a custodian's flat for the College.

THE OUTER LIBRARY

Steuart's most handsome room was already being altered in 1799. In order to accommodate the 2nd Lord Berwick's Italian purchases here, another library was fitted out in Tern Hall, when this room became known as the Museum. In the early 19th century Attingham was as famous for its Etruscan vases as for its paintings, and the 1827 sale catalogue listed 70 such vases along with other antiquities. To display these, alternate bays of the shelving were painted in a burnt umber, while the flanking white-painted bays probably continued to house books, and doors were fitted to the shelves beneath the dado.

Following the demolition of Tern Hall c.1856, the billiard-table was moved here and remained *in situ* until the room was required as a ward for the convalescent hospital in the First World War. The rings cut in the columns on the colonnade outside date from this period; they held the hammocks slung between the columns so that the patients could take the fresh air. This was the office for the agent of the estate from the 1930s until it was converted into a tea-room in the 1970s to cater for the increasing numbers of visitors to the house. It was redecorated in 1990 following colours found in the room, which correspond with Steuart's design for the library at Erlestoke in Wiltshire in 1785.

PICTURES

The grisaille paintings above the bookcases were installed later by the 2nd Lord Berwick, who must have commissioned them from Robert Fagan when he was in Italy.

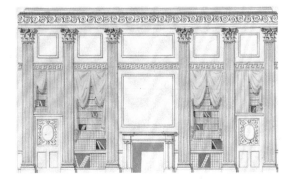

SCULPTURE

Lord Berwick purchased sculptures in Italy, commissioning copies of well-known pieces such as the Apollo Belvedere, carved for him by John Deare, or acquiring antiquities through the various dealers. His companion, Edward Clarke, observed 'the wonderful system of imposition and villainy that is practised here upon poor John Bull every hour in the day. The greatest of these Romans carry cheating to such a degree of ingenuity that it becomes a science.' Some of Lord Berwick's purchases were delayed in their passage by Napoleon's campaign in Italy, and some were impounded before they could be transported. Robert Fagan assisted Lord Berwick in securing the Apollo, which reached Malta in 1803 but did not arrive at Attingham until 1810.

In 1827 John Soane bought the cork model of an Etruscan tomb which is still in the Soane Museum. Edward Clarke's tufa model of Vesuvius, perhaps the most talked-about piece in Lord Berwick's collection, survived into the 20th century.

The National Trust is grateful to the Walker Art Gallery, Liverpool, for the loan of the sculpture displayed here.

CLOCK

Eight-day French mantel clock in ormolu portico case by Angevin, Paris, c.1830.

FURNITURE

Inlaid mahogany and satinwood plan chest, c.1810, a stylish piece that has been linked to the work of George Bullock.

Mahogany library steps, c.1790, purchased from Weston Park and similar to one of the three sets of steps described in the 1827 sale catalogue.

BOOKS

These include a large collection of 17th-century law books, some of which belonged to the 1st Lord Berwick's grandfather, Judge William Noel. A number of gifts have helped to fill the shelves, most notably from Dr Newsome, a bibliophile and amateur bookbinder.

(Left) Steuart's design for the chimneypiece wall of the Outer Library

The Outer Library

THE PARK

HISTORY

When John Byng rode past Attingham in 1784, his comments were far from flattering. He described the 'ugly grounds which are flat with small circular plantations'. This landscape had been laid out for the 1st Lord Berwick in 1770 by a little-known landscape gardener, Thomas Leggett. Leggett's ambitious project involved planting some 20,000 trees over two years and transforming the setting of the old Tern Hall from a formal garden to broad open parkland, with a solid screen of trees round the newly extended boundaries and isolated clumps in the intervening pastureland.

By the time Humphry Repton was called in by the 2nd Lord Berwick in 1797, Leggett's planting was ready for judicious thinning. Repton presented his proposals to the 2nd Lord Berwick in his customary 'Red Book', which is happily still at Attingham. The flat and essentially featureless nature of the Attingham landscape makes it easier to identify Repton's scheme and to admire his achievement in creating the seemingly natural, pastoral landscape that survives in essence today.

TOUR OF THE PLEASURE GROUNDS

FRONT LAWN AND APPROACHES

One of Repton's main themes was to relocate the drives, thereby expanding not just them, but also the image conveyed of Lord Berwick's ownership and wealth. Previously the drive had curved up the centre of the front lawn, but now the park was to be extended westwards to Atcham and a new impressive gateway built. This was designed by John Nash, who was Repton's partner at this time. Half-way along this drive, a group of oak trees was planted beside the pool, effectively screening the house and creating the sense of surprise and again of greater distance when the vast mansion finally comes into view.

From the portico of the house the views outwards were artfully revised by Repton. Leggett's solid boundary planting was opened up and focussed views created: south through the bridge to the river and hills beyond; eastwards to the Wrekin; and to the south-west, where the corner tower of Cronkhill is glimpsed (see p. 54). Repton's concern

Tern Bridge with Attingham in the distance; from Repton's Red Book

was to conceal the appearance of any boundary which might destroy the impression of his patron's limitless ownership.

WITHIN THE HA-HA

The immediate surroundings of Attingham probably represent the area of the private grounds of Tern Hall. The formal gardens lay between the house and the river, but the family's pleasure in the garden was marred by the proximity of the forge, situated on the river just below and generating noise throughout the day and night. Nevertheless, there was constant interest in the garden, with plants and horticultural advice being exchanged between Tern and the Hills' cousins at Hawkstone.

In the 1730s, when the property passed to Thomas Hill, new schemes for avenues and walks were put in hand. Plants and seeds were ordered from London and in 1733 the London garden designer Stephen Switzer paid a visit to advise on a kitchen garden. Hill's second marriage to Susanna Noel in 1740 brought renewed interest, although the family continued to spend most of their time in London. A bowling green was laid, probably in the area now occupied by the east pavilion, but by 1770 the formal terraces and walls were being taken down to open up views of the River Tern.

In the 1920s Lady Berwick, inspired by the Italian gardens of her childhood, reintroduced a formal scheme to this area. She sought advice from the garden designers Cecil Pinsent and Brenda Colvin, and created three yew-lined compartments as a setting for the house, those in front of the colonnades being filled with box-edged beds and colourful annuals. After the Second World War the cost of employing gardeners and the Trust's desire to reinstate Repton's landscape combined to sweep away this scheme.

The Greenhouse or Orangery, which occupies the east pavilion of Steuart's building, is balanced by the Outer Library in the west pavilion. Orangeries first became fashionable in England in the 1660s for overwintering citrus fruits. By the 1780s, when this example was built, glazed roofs were being introduced to allow more light for the increasing number of exotics being grown. Its use as an orangery was short-lived, and it became a store. In 1920 it was used as a cinema when the 8th Lord and Lady Berwick gave a party for the estate tenants, and in the 1950s it was converted into a maisonette for the warden of the College. It was restored as an orangery in 1992 thanks to a generous donation from the National Gardens Scheme.

The Cedar Grove was probably not planted until 1802 and is not mentioned in the Red Book, although in his published theory Repton recommended cedars specifically to provide a horizontal foil to the verticality of classical buildings.

TERN RIVER AND BRIDGES

This modest river was an important source of power, which was fully harnessed in the 18th century with three forges and corn mills operating along the one-mile stretch from the River Severn, within the Attingham estate. Tern Forge (see p. 42) was situated just below the present stone bridge of c.1800. The mound alongside the park bridge conceals a brick ice-house, soon to be repaired but currently closed to visitors. It is an unusual square plan with an outer passage providing extra insulation, and may have been designed by Nash. It was converted into a pump-house to direct water from the river up to the Hall. The ice would have been collected from the flood-plain opposite and, if well insulated, such an ice-house could provide safe storage for meat from one year to the next.

In 1780 Noel Hill moved the main London–Holyhead road further away from the house and contributed towards the cost of a new bridge, to provide an ornamental feature in the principal view from Attingham. The bridge was to form a focal element in Repton's later landscaping scheme, although his proposal to extend it and insert an extra arch for a carriageway was never executed. On his recommendation, however, the course of the river beyond the bridge was straightened and a weir installed so as to enhance the view of water through the arch of the bridge. The weir was designed by Nash, but subsequently destroyed by floods. The water in front of the house has reverted to the 'meandring brook' that Repton sought to enlarge.

THE MILE WALK

This walk was designed by Thomas Leggett in 1770 and forms a loop taking in the river and returning past the walled garden. Leggett supplied numerous flowering trees and shrubs, which must have been destined for these Pleasure Grounds. (*Copies of these bills can be seen in the Bothy.*)

Most of the trees and shrubs along the riverside walk are species that might have been planted in the 1770s. An exception is the 'Ravenna' pine grown from the seed of a tree thought to have been brought by the last Lady Berwick from Italy. The venerable trunk of an elderly Acacia conveys the air of antiquity for which these trees were admired in the 18th century. It was due to the vigilance of the 8th Lord Berwick that so many mature trees have survived along this walk and were saved from being felled to meet the wartime need for timber.

The great cedar which marks the point at which the Mile Walk leaves the river may belong to the 1802 batch. From this point the planting takes on a different character with a variety of rhododendrons, azaleas and camellias, some probably planted in the 1920s but added to recently. A formal circle of *Gleditsia triacanthos* was planted in memory of Gordon Miller, who was land agent to the 8th Lord and Lady Berwick for some 50 years.

A wooden seat encircles a great oak tree which marks another change of character. The path here is of hard stone, having been laid in the last war when military vehicles were parked in the woods. The tree-planting from here up to the Stables is mostly 20th-century, including the handsome *Abies grandis* whose elegant branches sweep down to the edge of the path. Although not available in Repton's time, they create the type of effect he admired.

THE WALLED GARDEN

This probably also formed part of Leggett's scheme, situated some distance from the house, as was customary, and on the edge of the park he was creating. His bill of 1770 includes a quantity of fruit trees for the walls and 160 apple trees of sixteen varieties for the adjoining orchard. The different varieties were selected to ripen over as long a period as possible, in order to ensure fresh apples for the table at any time of the year. Great quantities of vegetable seeds were ordered from the London firm of Harrison in the early 1800s. In the early days of the Shrewsbury Flower Show the Attingham garden regularly won prizes for vegetables.

The cottage attached to the wall is the Bothy, where the young unmarried gardeners lived. (*It now houses a small exhibition about the landscape, and serves as a base for schools working in the park.*) Attached to the north wall are an apple store, mushroom shed and boiler room. The last is linked to flues running through the walls so that they could be kept warm and protect the fruit from frost. At the far end were shelters for a cart and pony which used to take the produce to market every week. In the 1920s the walled garden was let as a market garden, and it was here that Percy Thrower did some of his early garden demonstrations for the BBC in the 1950s. The open south-facing lawn was also used for growing vegetables. The timber Bee House, designed to house sixteen straw skeps, dates from about 1810 and used to stand in the orchard. The full restoration of the Walled Garden awaits the necessary funding.

BACK DRIVE AND STABLES

The western strip of land now within the park walls was acquired by the Hills only in 1777. Beyond the ditch which crosses the drive half-way lay the remnants of the medieval village of Berwick Maviston, including at least four substantial houses. Of these, only the 14th-century Home Farm survives; the rest were swept away when the park was expanded. Ironically perhaps, it was from this ancient settlement that the 1st Baron Berwick took his title.

Steuart's Stables, built round a courtyard, contained stabling for 56 horses, with the internal fittings graded according to the value of the horses; the 1st Lord Berwick's racehorses had stalls adorned with fluted urns. Two wings of the courtyard have been converted into offices.

Attingham Park from Tern Bridge, from Repton's Red Book, showing his proposals for remodelling the park and diverting the river

DEER PARK

The Deer Park and the adjoining woodland were not actually purchased by the Hills until the late 1790s. Nevertheless Leggett's planting scheme of 1770 seems to have included the belt of trees along the ridge, which forms a significant feature in the view from the house.

Repton created a new driveway from the bridge beside the house south to the Tern Lodge gates. He also extended the park landscaping south of the road, again to reinforce Lord Berwick's stature as landowner, and made a carriage drive through the woods opposite Tern Lodge. An existing cottage south of the road achieved new prominence with the rerouting of the junction of the River Tern. Called Confluence Cottage, this building of *c.*1810 contains an elegant front parlour overlooking the River Severn, to which the family would have repaired for refreshments.

The area immediately beside Tern Lodge was the site of a wartime hospital, demolished only in the 1950s, when it was replanted with trees, as Repton had proposed. Other military encampments relating to the adjoining airfield stood within the Deer Park and along the eastern boundary, and some of the connecting concrete roads survive.

The herd of fallow deer may be descended from wild deer occupying the area at the time of emparkment. At present there are some 180, their numbers controlled by annual culling. The 8th Lord Berwick had a particular fondness for the deer and would visit them daily when at Attingham. At his request, his ashes lie under a monument in the Deer Park, in a glade at the northern end of the ridge opposite the house. The design was inspired by Constable's painting, *The Cenotaph to Joshua Reynolds*. The author L. P. Hartley, a family friend, helped to compose the inscription which describes this gentle man: 'His life added distinction to an honoured name, a generous and careful landlord, a patron and lover of the Arts, he studied to leave his inheritance a thing of beauty that posterity might enjoy.'

THE NOEL-HILLS OF ATTINGHAM

SIR ROWLAND HILL

The Hill family had been established in Shropshire as members of the gentry for several generations by the time Noel Hill set about building his great new house in 1783. Their ancestor in Tudor times, Sir Rowland Hill, was Lord Mayor of London in 1549 and took advantage of the Dissolution of the Monasteries to acquire land belonging to several abbeys in the area: Shrewsbury, Lilleshall and Haughmond. His fortune derived from trading in textiles, particularly abroad, and was increased by money-lending, not least to his monarch. In 1556

Sir Rowland Hill (1492?–1561), an ancestor of the Noel-Hills of Attingham, who devoted much of his fortune to charity

he purchased the property at Hawkstone, north of Shrewsbury, which was to remain the chief seat of the family until sold in 1906.

A contemporary said of Sir Rowland: 'Wheresoever a good dede was to be done for the common weal of his countrymen, he was ready to further the cause.' His benefactions included founding Shrewsbury's grammar school (now the town library).

THE HON. AND REV. RICHARD HILL

The fortune founded by Sir Rowland was further increased by his descendant Richard Hill, who inherited the Hawkstone property in 1700. He took deacon's orders, but instead of pursuing a career in the church, became tutor to Lord Hyde, son of the Earl of Rochester. Through this connection he came to the notice of the Earl of Ranelagh, then Paymaster to the Forces, who appointed him his Deputy. He was unusually honest and efficient for the time; only his father seems to have had doubts about the fortune he amassed: 'My son Dick makes money very fast: God send that he gets it honestly.' Diplomatic missions followed, firstly to the Elector of Bavaria in Brussels, and most successfully to Turin, where he succeeded in persuading the Duke of Savoy to join the Grand Alliance with Spain against France. Following this success, he retired and took Holy Orders; he was offered a bishopric and a baronetcy, but rejected both (though he secured the latter for the nephew who became his heir). Instead, he concentrated on husbanding his estates and developing Hawkstone as a fitting inheritance for the dynasty he was establishing. In 1701 he also commissioned a new home on his Atcham estate near Shrewsbury – Tern Hall. The agreement with the carpenter, John Parker, set out the details precisely: three storeys, 47 feet long, 30 feet broad and 34 feet high, with a slate roof. Curiously,

Richard Hill may never have visited his Shropshire estates, preferring to remain in London, where he had built a house in the grounds of the old palace in Richmond but also had quarters at Cleveland Court, close to St James's Palace.

Richard Hill never married and on his death in 1727 bequeathed his properties and considerable fortune to three nephews. Hawkstone went to Rowland Hill, and Shenstone in Staffordshire to Samuel Barbour. Tern Hall passed to his sister Margaret and her eldest son, Thomas Harwood.

(Above right) Hawkstone Park from the 1822 Hawkstone guidebook

(Right) Richard Hill of Hawkstone (1654–1727), who built Tern Hall and bequeathed it to his nephew, Thomas Harwood

41

Thomas Hill with his first wife, Anne Powys, and their young family, painted in 1730, the year they moved out of Tern Hall because of the noise from the nearby iron forge (Inner Library)

THOMAS HILL

Thomas Harwood and his younger brother, another Rowland, were brought up at Tern Hall, where their education was directed by their wealthy uncle. Thomas, who assumed the surname of Hill in 1712, was sent to Eton and then travelled on the Continent, for a time taking an apprenticeship in banking at Amsterdam. As well as financial acumen, he acquired fluent French and became such a Francophile that he employed three French servants to ensure that his own children imbibed the French language and culture at an early age. Later, the extent of his investments in that country resulted in a slight ambivalence over the rival political fortunes of France and England.

The expansion of the neighbouring ironworks, and the noise generated, rendered Tern an increasingly unsatisfactory home, and in 1730 the Harwoods moved out. Thomas, who was due to inherit the property, was disinclined to use the house on his occasional visits from London, and it was let for a year to an aunt. The inventory drawn up at this time identified 26 different rooms, including cellars and garrets.

Thomas Harwood, who changed his name to Hill on inheriting Tern Hall; painted by John Smibert (Inner Library)

When his first wife died in 1739, Thomas was left with two young daughters, his eldest son Richard having died at the age of ten, and four more sons having died in infancy. He remarried, his new wife Susanna being the daughter of Judge William Noel, MP for Stamford. Four more children followed, the last in 1745, and it was this son, Noel, the thirteenth child, who was to inherit when Thomas finally died in 1782 at the great age of 89. Through his many continental links Hill came to employ as tutor to his youngest boys a young Swiss man, John Fletcher, who was later one of the most revered of Methodist ministers. Fletcher's stern faith led him to address the Atcham congregation as 'ye adulterers and adulteresses', and did not find sympathy with Mrs Hill, although she was a close friend of John Wesley's future wife. To avoid his influence, the two boys were sent early to Cambridge, but Samuel, the elder and Thomas's pride and joy, came under other influences there. Samuel went on a drunken binge lasting 23 days and surrendered to 'all that Indulgence which young men are but too apt to enjoy, in a soft Bed, and a soft bedfellow'. He died in 1766 at the age of only 23, probably of syphilis.

Thomas had inherited Tern Hall in 1734, following his mother's death. Although he enjoyed entertaining his friends with 'le son agreable des verres de vin', he was an austere character and remained at all times a punctilious businessman, even when dealing with close friends and family. Relations with his less prodigal younger son, Noel, were always cool. In 1749 he became MP for Shrewsbury as part of a deal whereby the town was represented by two Whigs and the county went to the Tories. In fact, for business reasons, he was careful not to incline himself too much to either party.

Hill's caution extended to spending money, and it was his second wife and son who pressed for improvements to Tern Hall. Indeed his friend and agent, James Bonnell, commented, 'The people in Shropshire ... imagine you so rich but your manner of living is by no means generous in proportion to your income.' On the death of his cousin Samuel in 1758, Thomas had the option of moving to Shenstone, but his wife persuaded him to stay at Tern, where improvements were already in

Tern Hall, which remained unfinished when Thomas Hill gave up living here in 1768. This view shows the house about 1775, after modification by his son, but before the building of Attingham

hand following the demolition of the noisy forge in 1757. The garret rooms were done up for the children, and in 1759 payments were made to Thomas Farnolls Pritchard, a Shropshire joiner-cum-builder turned architect, for Grinshill stone, boards and slate. The following year he was 'surveying the building'. An entirely new building was being added to the front of the existing Tern Hall, providing a panelled dining parlour, hall and staircase and drawing-room, with bedchambers above. The rooms were largely complete, with the exception of the drawing-room, when Mrs Hill died in 1760. However, by then a problem had arisen over the height of the windows, with Hill's agent reporting that the drawing of the front elevation had been left in London and that Pritchard had had to draw another, 'which made him curse and swear a Great Deale'. It was not until 1764 that Pritchard's name again appears in the accounts, along with carpenters, plasterers, glaziers and a carver. Even so, the house remained unfinished in 1768, when Thomas Hill gave up living here.

NOEL, 1ST LORD BERWICK

In 1768 Tern Hall was given to Noel, Thomas's only surviving son, on his marriage to Anne Vernon, a granddaughter of the Earl of Strafford. This new alliance encouraged Noel Hill to spend the fortune so carefully garnered by his father on completing his mother's renovation of Tern Hall and on new projects. In 1771 Noel explained to his father that all the windows had had to be lowered, 'owing to the Blunder of an Architect who built the Windows so high from the Ground that no-one sitting could look out of them'. Although Noel Hill received Pritchard's designs for chimneypieces for the new rooms in 1769, by then he had lost confidence in his architect, and in the same year the name of Robert Mylne appears. Over the next four years, Mylne finally brought this troubled project to a conclusion. In 1775 Mylne also provided designs for a new stable block, gardener's house, greenhouse and cottage. Designs for a new lodge and a bridge were followed by further proposals for alterations to Tern Hall, which were not carried out. In 1777 Mylne also produced a scheme for the London house at Cleveland Court, which proved similarly abortive. At the same time, Noel Hill was also commissioning Thomas Leggett to make substantial alterations to the setting of the house, as evidenced by invoices listing several thousands of trees purchased. His father, who had moved to a house in Abbey Fore-gate in Shrewsbury, at first supported this work, but in due course he grew concerned and urged economies, accusing Noel of succumbing to 'the follies of the age'.

Meanwhile Noel was leading the busy life of the country squire, hunting and horse-racing being favourite pastimes. These contributed to his contingent of servants, as well as his costs, and in 1774 he was maintaining fourteen menservants, from steward to dog-feeder, not to mention the many female servants required to run the house and attend to his wife and their six children. Noel hoped that his father had enjoyed his visit in 1778 'pretty well ... and that the Children are not too noisy for you'.

In 1768 Thomas had relinquished his seat as MP for Shrewsbury in favour of Noel. However, in 1774 Noel was able to secure the support of his friends in Shropshire to become MP for the county. In 1784 he won the Prime Minister Pitt the Younger's lasting gratitude and a title for supporting him on the East India Bill.

In 1782 his father died at the great age of 89. Just seven months later, work started on the building of his vast new house, to be called Attingham in an antiquarian reference to the medieval name of the village of Atcham. Like his parents just fifteen years previously, Noel added to, rather than demolished, the existing house, which remained in use until the 1850s, choosing the Scot George Steuart as his architect. He may already have seen Steuart's unexecuted designs of 1779 for nearby Onslow Hall, which belonged to a cousin, Rowland Wingfield. Steuart's first designs for Onslow show some of the hallmarks of his work: a somewhat austere main block with the central portico attached almost as an afterthought. The attenuated pilasters of the side elevations of Attingham are repeated at Erlestoke in Wiltshire and a later scheme for Onslow, as are the windows set in recessed arches, which are such a feature of the pavilions and stable block at Attingham. The steward noted that 120 workmen were engaged on site in 1784, and the following year recorded on 8 October: 'My Lord dined in ye new House, Attingham ye first time.' Two days later, 'Lady Berwick slept in ye new house ye first time'. But the interiors were probably incomplete when Lord Berwick died four years later, and his children certainly continued to occupy rooms in the old Tern Hall.

Noel, 1st Lord Berwick, the builder of Attingham; miniature by Jeremiah Meyer (East Ante-Room)

The elongated columns and lack of decoration are typical of George Steuart's plain Neo-classical style

As the only one of Steuart's domestic buildings to survive relatively intact, Attingham takes on additional interest. The quality of the stonework and construction is outstanding, and may be due to John White, a London surveyor whose surviving notebook suggests that he was a contractor or surveyor for the project. The austere Neo-classicism of the exterior, the symmetrical plan with its French nuances in the layout and the extraordinary variety, and in some cases originality, of the ceiling designs – all these combine to confirm Steuart's status as a significant architect of his period. The Palladian plan with outlying wings, which might be deemed old-fashioned at this date, was one which he continued to adopt at Erlestoke and Barons Court, and on the later schemes for Onslow. At Attingham the recessed outflung wings were in part necessitated by the need to enclose the existing building of Tern Hall. Steuart redesigned the interiors of Tern Hall in order to integrate them with his new plan. Indeed, these redesigned rooms, which included a marble-lined bath installed by Joseph Bromfield in 1802, may have been more fully used than those of the new house. A second dining-room overlooking the west colonnade was more convenient for the kitchen below, while the adjoining billiard-room was hung with an impressive collection of landscapes by Claude, Hackert, Daniell, Canaletto and Orizzonte.

At the same time that work at Attingham was progressing, Noel was also commissioning major refurbishments to his new London house in fashionable Portman Square. Steuart was also employed here, principally in redecoration, in which role he had begun his career, sometimes working for Robert Adam, who was predictably put out when he became an architect. The lavish improvements in London had a purpose, for in 1784 a great masquerade was held there. Amongst the guests was the Prince of Wales, whose party came disguised as 'a convent of grey friars'. This was the circle in which the Hills now moved, a link which developed with the relationship between the Prince and Mrs Fitzherbert, who was the niece of Mr Errington, Noel's sister's second husband. That same year saw Noel's advancement to a barony, thus outstripping his cousins at Hawkstone in status as well as in the scale of his new house. His motto QUI UTI SCIT EI BONA was selected from the Roman playwright Terence by his former tutor at Cambridge. This somewhat worldly, but highly appropriate, motto can be translated as 'let wealth be his who knows its use'.

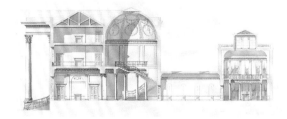

Steuart's cutaway view of Attingham, showing the portico, Entrance Hall, central staircase (replaced by the Picture Gallery), and Outer Library. An unexecuted scheme

THOMAS, 2ND LORD BERWICK

In 1789 Lord Berwick died at the early age of 43. He was succeeded by his eldest son, Thomas, who was only nineteen at the time and was to be the first of three brothers who in turn succeeded to the title and estate. In 1792 Thomas set off for Italy in the company of Edward Clarke, who had been a contemporary at Cambridge and who was to go on to become a noted geologist and professor at that university. According to his memoirs, it was he who guided Lord Berwick's taste and purchases, which were considerable. In Rome he commissioned sculpture from John Deare and three paintings from Angelica Kauffman, including his own portrait. For the winter he travelled on to Naples, where he

Thomas, 2nd Lord Berwick, painted in 1793 in Rome in 'Van Dyck' fancy dress by Angelica Kauffman. His extravagance led to bankruptcy and the sale of the contents of Attingham in 1827 (Drawing Room)

seems to have spent a whole year, visiting archaeological sites and enjoying the social life which revolved around Sir William Hamilton and his wife Emma.

His mother and three sisters had joined him in Naples and indeed Lady Berwick was to spend all her widowhood abroad, as she had not been left sufficiently well-off to maintain an independent establishment in London. An acquaintance in Italy found her 'very amiable and gay'. She achieved a successful match for one of her daughters in Italy, when Henrietta married Lord Bruce, later 1st Marquess of Ailesbury.

On his return to England, the 2nd Lord Berwick was soon embroiled in Shropshire politics, for his brother William, aged just 23, had decided to stand for election as MP for Shrewsbury. In so doing, he was competing against his kinsman and the family trustee, Sir John Hill of Hawkstone. This notorious election of 1796, in which the parties are said to have spent £100,000 on ale for voters, was finally resolved by the Mayor, who declared William Hill the winner. William went on to represent Shrewsbury until 1812, when he was bribed by his brother not to stand again, since the cost of the campaigns had severely depleted the family fortune.

Meanwhile, Thomas had embarked on improvements and alterations to Attingham to accommodate his purchases in Italy. The Outer Library was converted into a museum for the display of sculpture, Etruscan vases and a model of Vesuvius. New bookcases were installed in the former breakfast-room, and Gillows provided new curtains in all the principal rooms, along with a considerable quantity of bedroom furniture. The chief alteration, however, was the insertion of the great Picture Gallery in the centre of the house, a scheme designed by John Nash and said by admiring visitors to have cost £7,000. Nash had already secured commissions from the 2nd Lord Berwick through his partnership with Repton, and his relationship with this patron obviously prospered, for he went on to carry out another commission for him in 1812 on his London house in Grosvenor Square. In devising the scheme for the Gallery, it may seem surprising that Nash did not use the space offered by the older rooms in Tern Hall. However, the chosen

The Picture Gallery was built by Nash to display the great collection of Old Master and modern paintings and sculpture the 2nd Lord Berwick had acquired on the Grand Tour in Italy; the skylights were built to a different design

location links this splendid new addition directly to the principal rooms of the main floor, and indeed the scale of the Gallery accommodates well with its surroundings.

In designing the Picture Gallery, both Nash and his patron would have been well aware of the contemporary discussion and theories relating to galleries – chiefly the lighting, but also the design and decoration. At this date the picture gallery had become a fashionable addition, with picture collections expanding as a result of travels abroad, the auctions of French collections due to the Revolution, and the success of the new Royal Academy in promoting British art. At Attingham, just as in the contemporary picture galleries built for Thomas Hope and Sir John Leicester in London, top lighting was adopted as the best method of illuminating paintings. However, Nash's scheme for lighting the Picture Gallery at Attingham is unique. Discarding his original proposal for great oval openings in the cove, perhaps for technical reasons, he opted for a continuous cove of glazed panels. These are made up of small panes of glass set in a cast-iron frame, with secondary glazing above, and attached to cast-iron beams which support the roof, the latter made at Coalbrookdale. The curvature ensures that the light falls over a wide area, so that the lower pictures are better lit than by the more customary lantern-style roof-lighting. However, the many small panes,

lightly etched to diffuse the light, give greater opportunity for leaks, which certainly proved to be a continuous problem, with major repairs already arising in 1807. A second glazed roof was installed in the 1960s, replacing a previous attempt at resolving this fundamental design flaw.

As the new Picture Gallery was only one and a half storeys high, some of Steuart's previously internal walling was now exposed above the roof. Nash's solution, in order to add the minimum of weight, was to face these walls with mathematical tiles, which give the illusion of a brick façade. The new wall built behind the screen of columns in the Entrance Hall is a further acknowledgement of the concern for the weight being created by the new roof construction.

The Picture Gallery was Thomas's last extravagant gesture – unless his marriage can be so described. For in 1812 at the age of 42 he made a quite unsuitable match with a seventeen-year-old, Sophia Dubouchet. The daughter of a Swiss clockmaker, she was one of four sisters who carried on the profession of courtesan in the frenetic social world surrounding the Prince of Wales. Lord Berwick was obviously infatuated and pursued her with such determination that she was finally and reluctantly persuaded to marry him. The marriage brought social isolation, further extravagance and no happiness. As her sister, Harriette Wilson, recalled, 'Sophia, having the command of more guineas than ever she had expected to have had pence, did nothing, from morning till night, but throw them away.'

In 1810 Lord Berwick himself admitted to his brother 'not having resolution to abstain from Building and Picture buying'. The family's finances deteriorated, while the brothers bickered about who was to blame. Finally, Lord Berwick was declared bankrupt, and in 1827 a sixteen-day auction took place at Attingham, in which the entire contents of the house were sold. The sale catalogue records a great house furnished in lavish fashion at the height of the Regency period, but only a few items of furniture and paintings bought in by the family still remain at Attingham today. The auction did not raise enough to settle all the debts, and Lord Berwick retired to Italy, where he died in 1832.

WILLIAM, 3RD LORD BERWICK

In the meantime, his brother William took a lease of Attingham, which in due course he inherited along with the title. He brought to Attingham the collections of furniture and pictures, ceramics and silver that he had accumulated during some 25 years as a diplomat in Italy. His career had begun in 1807, when he was appointed minister at Ratisbon, a position which he never took up owing to Napoleon's campaign. His next appointment to the Court of Savoy was similarly disrupted by Napoleon and he first joined the Court at Cagliari in Sardinia. He described his diplomatic role as being largely concerned with 'losses of Bonnets & Gowns, cruel Custom House officers or the want of Passports', but he was a natural bon viveur and enjoyed the role of entertaining some of the English travellers in

(Above, left) William, 3rd Lord Berwick, who rescued Attingham after his brother's bankruptcy and collected many of the paintings and furniture now at Attingham while in Italy (Dining Room)

(Above) Henrietta Noel-Hill, the elder sister of the 2nd, 3rd and 4th Lords Berwick; painted by Sir Thomas Lawrence (Dining Room)

Italy. Among these was Lord Byron, *en route* for Greece, who described him as 'the only one of the diplomatists whom I ever knew who really is *Excellent*'.

In 1824 William was transferred to Naples as Minister Plenipotentiary to the Court of the Two Sicilies. Finding his predecessor's accommodation unsuited to his own lavish lifestyle, he leased the Palazzo Belvedere, which had been furnished by Caroline Murat, the former Queen of Naples, in the latest French fashion. The furniture and Parisian ceramics and ormolu that Lord Berwick acquired with the Palazzo Belvedere now form a significant part of the furnishing and character of Attingham, along with the pictures which he had collected throughout his time in Italy.

RICHARD, 4TH LORD BERWICK

Although he had two children, the 3rd Lord Berwick never married so that on his death in 1842 the title passed to the third brother, Richard. He had entered the Church in 1799 and a year later had married Frances Mostyn-Owen. A new rectory was built for him at Berrington on the Attingham estate, where he enjoyed the life of a country squire. Like his brothers, he was incapable of economy, prompting Thomas to describe him as 'so very idle & extravagant of his wife, indolent & ignorant of management'. A severe speech impediment, which also affected other members of the family, must have made preaching difficult. Although already 68 when he inherited, he nevertheless moved into Attingham, with his several unmarried daughters. Apparently, he did not entertain, but is said to have 'swallowed more wine than any other man in the County'.

Richard, 4th Lord Berwick, who lived the quiet life of a rector and country squire before he inherited Attingham at the age of 68

Christ expelling the Money-changers from the Temple; by Salvator Rosa (Picture Gallery) One of the 3rd Lord Berwick's acquisitions

RICHARD, 5TH LORD BERWICK

Richard, 5th Lord Berwick

The 4th Lord Berwick did not get on with his eldest son, another Richard, who had set up a separate establishment at Cronkhill, a villa on the estate (see p. 54). As a young man he had acted as secretary to his uncle while in Italy, and was recommended for a career in the Foreign Office. He opted instead for the life of a country squire. He took a mistress, but never married and chose not to move into Attingham when he inherited the property in 1848. By carefully husbanding his resources, he cleared off the estate's debts and in 1857 was able to commission a programme of major repairs, not only renewing slate roofs and leadwork and some chimneys, but also making massive structural alterations. These included demolishing what remained of the old Tern Hall, despite the fact that he seems to have had his rooms in the old house. All that remained were the three outer walls that had been subsumed into the new building, and some of the vaulted basement rooms. Only partial redevelopment took place, with the creation of new passages in the basement linking the wings to the main house, and the building of the new kitchen.

The 5th Lord Berwick developed one of the first herds of Hereford cattle, winning prizes in England and abroad. The impressive new model farm buildings at Lower Brompton were built to accommo-date his herd, as well as the American trotters which were his other interest, and which he imported himself from the United States. Portraits of some of his prize stock now hang in the West Pavilion. The 5th Lord Berwick was not only an accomplished musician, but also made flutes and clarinets in his own workshop. The same practical talents led him to construct agricultural instruments and to design his own rifle, which was patented as the Cronkhill in 1860.

(Left) One of the Hereford cattle bred by the 5th Lord Berwick at Attingham

(Right) William, 6th Lord Berwick

WILLIAM, 6TH LORD BERWICK

The second brother, William Noel, was almost 60 when he inherited the title and estate in 1861. Like his elder brother, he never married, and maintained a separate establishment at Springfield House in Sutton, on the outskirts of Shrewsbury, then still part of the Attingham estate. He had entered the army at the early age of fifteen, joining the 87th Foot. He served in the Burmese War of 1825–6 and retired in 1854 as a Colonel.

He used to stay at Attingham occasionally and entertained there with his sisters. On such occasions he evidently maintained a full household of staff, perhaps importing some from Springfield House, for the 1871 census records no fewer than seventeen live-in servants. Sir Baldwin Leighton, a neighbour, reported 'the present Lord … is more sociable and has asked us [to Attingham] several times…. The house is probably the largest in the County and it must be very dreary for the owner living there alone. Owing to incompatibility of temper he and his sister Emily are unable to reside together.' To

Richard, 7th Lord Berwick

another visitor, Attingham was a melancholy place: 'The rooks were cawing their vespers on the elms, and the old hall, with but one small lamp burning faintly in its regiment of windows, stood out gaunt and drear in the twilight.'

RICHARD, 7TH LORD BERWICK

One of the 6th Baron's twin nephews became the 7th Baron Berwick in 1882. Richard Henry Noel-Hill was brought up at Berrington Rectory, where his father, Thomas Noel-Hill, was Rector. Debt forced the young Dick Hill to leave the army, and he was rumoured to have married a Mrs Norton, 'a lady of the town' aged over 30. In fact that year he married Ellen Nystrom, a member of an old Swedish family in Malmö. The 7th Lord Berwick was a sailor, and he and his wife lived for periods on his yacht, the *Clio*. When at Attingham, shooting was his chief interest, and even when illness prevented him from walking, he would have himself taken out in a donkey cart for a day's sport.

THOMAS, 8TH LORD BERWICK

Like so many of his predecessors, the 7th Lord Berwick produced no heirs. He was succeeded by his nephew, the son of his twin brother, who, continuing a family tradition, was Rector of Berrington. Thomas Henry Noel-Hill was orphaned at the age of eleven, and he and his sister Mary were brought up by their aunt at Cronkhill. He entered the diplomatic service in 1903 and was posted to Paris, where he developed a profound interest in French decorative arts, which resulted in numerous purchases for Attingham. He met his future wife while serving in Italy during the First World War. Teresa Hulton, who married the 8th Lord Berwick in Venice in 1919, had been brought up in that city and had worked with the Italian army throughout the war, receiving the Croce di Guerra for her service. Her father was a painter, whose artist friends included Sickert and Sargent, whilst her mother was half-Italian and brought links with the literary and artistic community of Florence, including the Brownings and Berensons.

Lord and Lady Berwick initially planned to live at Cronkhill and to let Attingham, which had already been leased since 1903. However, after the First World War, it proved impossible to find tenants for the great house, so their plans were reversed. In fact Attingham proved more convenient, having the advantages of electric lighting and some heating. The last tenants, the Van Bergen family, who were referred to as 'the margerine people', had brought Canadian standards of modern life to some aspects of Attingham, re-equipping the laundry, the kitchen and providing heating for the servants' rooms. However, the main rooms were in a state of sad neglect, because the house had been used as a hospital and had so little spent on it over the preceding 50 years.

Together, Lord and Lady Berwick gradually achieved a renaissance of the interiors, bringing to the task their very particular interests. Before the war, Lord Berwick had already purchased French furniture and silk damasks, and he continued to make thoughtful additions to the collection, such as the portrait of Caroline Murat and the two Canova statues. By contrast, Lady Berwick was ever conscious of the need for economies. She repaired silk hangings and upholstery, reusing old damask and silks found in store. To fund these improvements, they sold silver and Carpaccio's *Holy Family* (now in the Gulbenkian Collection). A new continental influence prevailed even on the farm, where the calves were named Picasso,

(Far left) Thomas, 8th Lord Berwick, who, with his wife, brought Attingham back to life

(Left) Teresa, Lady Berwick, painted by Sir Gerald Kelly in 1923. According to James Lees-Milne, it shows her 'as she wished to be shown and became, a stately, middle-aged, English peeress'

Gauguin and Matisse. This was probably the live-liest period in the history of the house, and the visitors' book records regular house parties during the summer months. Guests included Italian and diplomatic connections, and several artists, writers and musicians, suggesting a more cosmopolitan and artistic ambience than might be expected in the heart of Shropshire.

All this ended with the onset of the Second World War, which brought dramatic changes to Attingham. An airfield was built to the east of the park, with related encampments, including a hospi-tal erected in rows of Nissan huts in the park itself. The house was at first used as a refuge by Edgbaston Church of England Girls School, prompting Lord Haw Haw to announce that the Church of England had evacuated to a house in Shropshire. With the arrival of the airfield, it was felt that the girls were as safe in Birmingham, and the house was taken over as offices by Pearl Assurance. Lastly, it was requisi-tioned by the WAAF. Lord and Lady Berwick remained in residence for most of this period, occu-pying rooms on the east side of the house.

In 1937 Lord Berwick had opened negotiations with the National Trust, being concerned to ensure the preservation of the house and park which he had devoted much of his life to restoring. In this he was able to take advantage of the 1937 National Trust Act, which enabled the Trust to accept land for its investment value (as in the case of an estate) rather than for its outstanding landscape value. James Lees-Milne, the National Trust representa-tive who negotiated the gift, described his first visit to the house in 1936:

It was always a slightly daunting experience to pedal through the lodge gates of a pompous country house…. Then a long drive was calculated to inspire awe. Then on arrival at the great portico, particularly if the weather were wet – on this occasion it was raw, foggy and wet – it could be humiliating having to strip off one's oilskin … under the supercilious gaze of a bevy of footmen. Luckily there were no footmen at Attingham. I do not remember there even being a butler. The Berwicks lived in this enormous palace in the utmost simplicity – from necessity.

Lord Berwick's bequest of Attingham, one of the most generous the Trust had received, was accom-

George Trevelyan enthusing a group of students in the Dining Room

panied by a Memorandum of Wishes in which he set out his hopes for the future.

In 1946 Shropshire County Council leased the whole house, apart from a few private rooms, for use as an adult education college. Under the charis-matic wardenship of George Trevelyan, the college was hugely successful during the post-war years of educational optimism. When cuts in the County Council's budget led to the closure of the college, Concorde College from Acton Burnell took on a lease as an annex for its many foreign students. Finally, that college too was forced to retrench, and the National Trust decided to restore and open more rooms to the public. Now the Trust's Regional Office occupies the back of the house, two flats take up part of the upper floors, but much of the basement and part of the first floor have been set aside for restoration.

In recent years major repairs have been carried out to the roofs and the portico, with the renewal of much of the lead. Some more exposed sections of the chimneys and pavilion balustrades have required replacement, and the National Trust has been fortunate to obtain sandstone from the same Grinshill quarry that supplied Lord Berwick in 1782.

THE ESTATE

Attingham lies in the north-west corner of an estate extending to some 1,500 hectares (3,707 acres), bisected by the serpentine passage of the River Severn. Now comprising mostly arable land, this estate was acquired by the National Trust not for its outstanding landscape value but for its traditional role of providing the income to maintain the great house and park at its core. The estate had already been reduced by sales in the 19th and early 20th centuries, chiefly of land to the west where the Hills' property formerly extended into the present outskirts of Shrewsbury, as well as land in Staffordshire.

The estate was built up by the succeeding members of the Hill family during the 18th century, beginning with the manor of Attingham (alias Atcham) in 1700. In fact, land lying east of the River Tern was purchased only in 1797, although the nearest section had already been leased and included in the park landscape by Thomas Leggett. The last part of the present estate to be acquired was the easternmost section at Uckington, which was purchased in 1808. In addition, the family owned a number of properties in Shrewsbury, particularly in the Abbey Foregate and Coleham areas, and including a small spa at Sutton.

CRONKHILL

The Regency villa at Cronkhill was built in 1802 for the 2nd Lord Berwick's agent, Francis Walford, by Nash, who was probably also responsible for the adjoining model farm. It stands on the highest point on the estate, and was intended to create an eye-catcher, visible from Attingham and the park. The result was one of Nash's most original buildings, which may have been inspired by the Claude landscapes in Lord Berwick's collection. It has been called 'the architectural essence of the Picturesque movement'. Nash refaced an existing 17th-century timber-framed farmhouse in brick to form a long wing balancing his circular and square towers. The arcade, which contributes so much to the picturesque and Italianate qualities of the exterior, frames spectacular views of the River Severn and the Wrekin. (*Cronkhill is privately tenanted, but has limited opening arrangements.*)

VILLAGES

In the village of Atcham, which lies at the entrance to the Park, all the property along the edge of the road used to belong to the estate. The name of Atcham has Saxon origins, translating as 'dwelling of the people of St Eata', suggesting that the community existed before the saint's death in 686. Like other early buildings in the area, the church of St Eata (the only church to bear that designation) contains vestiges of Roman stone, presumably taken from Wroxeter.

In the church hang the hatchments of both the Berwicks and the neighbouring Burton family

Cronkhill, the pioneer of the Picturesque villa in Britain

One of Nash's / A. C. Pugin's designs for a picturesque village at Atcham facing the gates to the park, c.1798

of Longner, who also own part of the village. It was the 1st Lord Berwick, however, who in 1775 rebuilt the handsome inn, then called the Talbot, for William Bennett, who had been promoted from footman (see p. 28) to butler. Its position took advantage of the newly rebuilt Atcham Bridge, which was designed by John Gwynne of Shrewsbury.

A drawing of the village of Atcham around 1790 shows a thriving community, including a blacksmith shop, glebe cottages and a substantial school house, all of which lie to the north of the main road. These were gradually demolished following Humphry Repton's scheme for the expansion of the park with a new entrance in Atcham. This involved the rerouting of the road northwards to Berwick Wharf, which had in fact only just been realigned following Leggett's scheme. The new entrance was designed by John Nash, whose imposing archway is angled to suggest that the bridge and the main road from Shrewsbury are directed to Attingham.

Around 1798 Nash also produced designs for a group of picturesque cottages at the gate of Attingham, of which one terrace with a distinctive Gothic bay window appears to have been built. A neighbouring 17th-century thatched cottage was probably gothicised at the same time. The Picturesque tradition was maintained in subsequent building along the road opposite the park, lastly with the neo-Gothic school and schoolhouse of 1866.

ROMAN WROXETER

A recent archaeological survey, together with aerial photography, have provided evidence of earlier activity on the estate. The eastern boundary abuts on to the perimeter of the Roman city of Viroconium (now Wroxeter), which was the fourth largest city in Roman Britain. Roman roads, cemeteries, marching camps, a fort and several pottery kilns have been discovered all lying to the east of the River Tern. To the north of the park, crop marks forming two large rectilinear outlines have been related to comparable sites thought to represent the outline of a Saxon palace. To protect these areas, in some cases, modern farming practices have been adapted, and the most sensitive areas have recently been put down to grass.

THE NOEL-HILLS OF ATTINGHAM

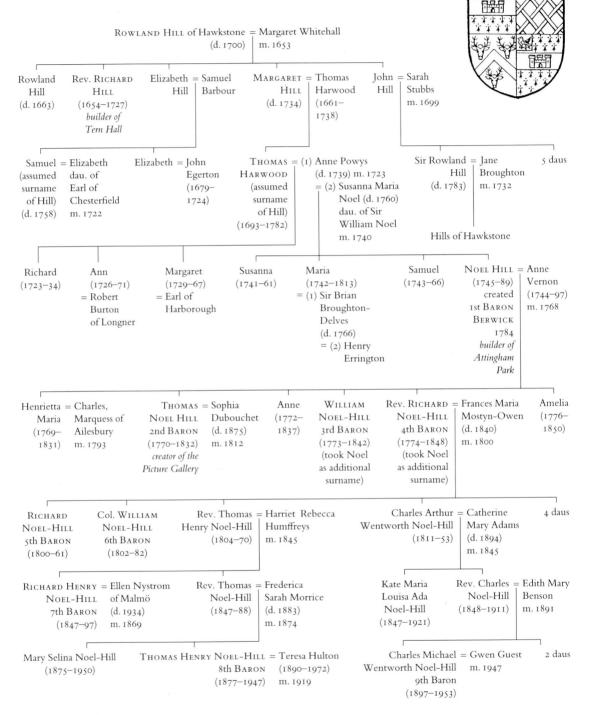

ROWLAND HILL of Hawkstone = Margaret Whitehall
(d. 1700) │ m. 1653

Rowland Hill (d. 1663)

Rev. RICHARD HILL (1654–1727) *builder of Tern Hall*

Elizabeth Hill = Samuel Barbour

MARGARET HILL (d. 1734) = Thomas Harwood (1661–1738)

John Hill = Sarah Stubbs m. 1699

Samuel (assumed surname of Hill) (d. 1758) = Elizabeth dau. of Earl of Chesterfield m. 1722

Elizabeth = John Egerton (1679–1724)

THOMAS HARWOOD (assumed surname of Hill) (1693–1782) = (1) Anne Powys (d. 1739) m. 1723 = (2) Susanna Maria Noel (d. 1760) dau. of Sir William Noel m. 1740

Sir Rowland Hill (d. 1783) = Jane Broughton m. 1732

5 daus

Hills of Hawkstone

Richard (1723–34)

Ann (1726–71) = Robert Burton of Longner

Margaret (1729–67) = Earl of Harborough

Susanna (1741–61)

Maria (1742–1813) = (1) Sir Brian Broughton-Delves (d. 1766) = (2) Henry Errington

Samuel (1743–66)

NOEL HILL (1745–89) created 1st BARON BERWICK 1784 *builder of Attingham Park* = Anne Vernon (1744–97) m. 1768

Henrietta Maria (1769–1831) = Charles, Marquess of Ailesbury m. 1793

THOMAS NOEL HILL 2nd BARON (1770–1832) *creator of the Picture Gallery* = Sophia Dubouchet (d. 1875) m. 1812

Anne (1772–1837)

WILLIAM NOEL-HILL 3rd BARON (1773–1842) (took Noel as additional surname)

Rev. RICHARD NOEL-HILL 4th BARON (1774–1848) (took Noel as additional surname) = Frances Maria Mostyn-Owen (d. 1840) m. 1800

Amelia (1776–1850)

RICHARD NOEL-HILL 5th BARON (1800–61)

Col. WILLIAM NOEL-HILL 6th BARON (1802–82)

Rev. Thomas Henry Noel-Hill (1804–70) = Harriet Rebecca Humffreys m. 1845

Charles Arthur Wentworth Noel-Hill (1811–53) = Catherine Mary Adams (d. 1894) m. 1845

4 daus

RICHARD HENRY NOEL-HILL 7th BARON (1847–97) = Ellen Nystrom of Malmö (d. 1934) m. 1869

Rev. Thomas Noel-Hill (1847–88) = Frederica Sarah Morrice (d. 1883) m. 1874

Kate Maria Louisa Ada Noel-Hill (1847–1921)

Rev. Charles Noel-Hill (1848–1911) = Edith Mary Benson m. 1891

Mary Selina Noel-Hill (1875–1950)

THOMAS HENRY NOEL-HILL 8th BARON (1877–1947) = Teresa Hulton (1890–1972) m. 1919

Charles Michael Wentworth Noel-Hill 9th Baron (1897–1953) = Gwen Guest m. 1947

2 daus

Owners of Attingham in CAPITALS

56